C000262076

# TIMES AND SEASONS
# OF THE SOUL

MAUREEN WOOD

CROSSBOOKS
PUBLISHING

CrossBooks™
A Division of LifeWay
One LifeWay Plaza
Nashville, TN 37234
www.crossbooks.com
Phone: 1-866-768-9010

Scripture taken from the Holman Christian Standard Bible ® Copyright © 2003, 2002, 2000, 1999 by Holman Bible Publishers. All rights reserved.

First published by CrossBooks  12/19/2014

ISBN: 978-1-4627-5586-8 (sc)
ISBN: 978-1-4627-5585-1 (e)

Library of Congress Control Number: 2014920090

Printed in the United States of America.

This book is printed on acid-free paper.

# CONTENTS

Introduction ........................................................ vii

Chapter 1 ............................................................ 1

Chapter 2 ........................................................... 11

Chapter 3 ........................................................... 15

Chapter 4 ........................................................... 20

Chapter 5 ........................................................... 25

Chapter 6 ........................................................... 32

Chapter 7 ........................................................... 36

Chapter 8 ........................................................... 45

Chapter 9 ........................................................... 57

Chapter 10 .......................................................... 66

# INTRODUCTION

The grace of the Lord Jesus Christ can never be fathomed. Norman, my husband and I know that grace was extended to us personally when Jesus Christ became our Lord and Savior. Norman in Rhodesia (now Zimbabwe) and myself, Maureen in South Africa.

We discovered that according to Ecclesiastics, in the Old Testament of the Bible, there is an occasion for everything under heaven which is appropriate and helpful to us, even those things that appear to be negative instead of positive. These are NOT curses and obstacles; they are God's blessings. Even our enemies are a blessing. ***"Love your enemies and pray for those who persecute you"***, *Jesus said,* in Matthew 5:44 HCSB.

Too often we have a shallow concept of things. We want everything to be smooth and pleasant, but more than that, we want to extend joy, pleasure, and have a smooth and uncomplicated quality of life.

Jesus said: HCSB John 10:10 *"I have come that they may have life and that they may have it in abundance.*

There is a quality in life for all humanity, which can never be explained by rationale and as a consequence we struggle with the sovereignty of God and the life He gives us. We are meant to be enjoying life but instead we do not and that is because we have never learned to accept the truth of Paul in HCSB Romans 8:28 *We know that all things work together, for good to those who love God those who are called according to His purpose"* not some things, not many things, not most things, BUT **ALL** things work together for our good.

Once we grasp that we, like the writer of Ecclesiastes are growing in our knowledge. We discover that the more we know, the more we realize that there is more yet that we need to know. The increase of knowledge only increases the depth of wonder and delight of our eternal Father.

There were times of rejoicing in the 'good events' of life and also a time of knowing that He was always in control in the 'bad' times. During the bad times He showed us that Philippians 4:19 HCSB *And my God shall supply all your needs according to His riches in glory in Christ Jesus"* This is so His purposes and His plans may be accomplished.

*There is a time to give birth and a time to die"* Ecclesiastes 3:2. HCSB. None of us asked to be born; it happened apart from us. None of us asks to die; it is something God determines. We are told that we can have choices and responses which we can make to all our times. It also says there is "*a time to weep and a time to laugh, a time to mourn and a time to dance*". Ecclesiastes 3:4 HCSB All these things follow closely, and they are all appropriate. No one is going to escape the hurts and sorrows of this life. In a fallen world it is true that there will be times of hurt, of sorrow and weeping.

# Chapter 1

Ecclesiastes 3 Verse 2: HCSB "*...a time to give birth ...*"

South Africa is the country of Maureen's, birth. I was born just in time to embark on a journey which enabled me to see drastic changes take place in South Africa. The characters that came onto the scene were not heroes from a book, but real flesh and blood people. The recording seems all the more urgent because the incidents and events would otherwise be lost as I try to recall some of them with the passing of time.

The lush subtropical forests, deserts of South Africa's western coast, sparkling, beaches and her cloud-capped mountain ranges are glorious, South Africa presents an ever-changing pattern of contrasts. The treasures of her underground mineral wealth are equaled only by the richness of her animal life and the diversity of her peoples.

My father Albert Edward Wade was a foreman on a gold mine. Working with him were two men, who, later became significant in our lives. Gary Player a world renowned golfer

1

had a father who worked with my father. The Grandfather of our future son-in-law, Wayne, also worked with my father.

At the age of fifteen I was 'born again' of the Spirit of God when I accepted Jesus Christ as my Savior. I was called by God's Holy Spirit to enter the Bible Institute of Southern Africa in the year 1958-1959 to study the Scriptures and upon graduation to go to the mission field.

Onto this scene of the Bible Institute in Kalk Bay, Capetown, South Africa and into my life came … Norman Wood! His family immigrated to Rhodesia when he was three years old. He did all his schooling in Rhodesia (now Zimbabwe). Norman was born in Stonehaven, Scotland on October 23, 1935. Norman had been brought to faith in 1955 through a young preacher, Andrew van den Aardweg.

Ron Filby, a missionary came to speak at a family camp that same Easter. He challenged Norman concerning full-time ministry. His call began with a challenge to study the Word of God. The Bible Institute of Southern Africa in Cape Town was his starting point and we met there and fell in love.

Kalk Bay, Cape Town, was a beautiful spot to conduct our courtship. For two years we experienced all the changes of the climate, sea and mountains along with all the spiritual challenges during our courtship. We courted with the background of some of the most beautiful scenery anywhere in the world. One of the most famous mountains called Table Mountain almost always has cloud cover and is like a table beautifully draped with a table cloth and can be seen as one enters the Cape Town harbor. Norman was in fact lost up on one of those mountain trips for three days because of the rain and mist. The Cape is famous for its history. The Flemish and other European peoples came and settled there during the religious persecution of Protestants in Europe during the 16th Century.

We had two wonderful years at the Bible Institute under the most inspirational staff. Howard Green, an Englishman was one of the full-time lecturers. The then President was a Scotsman -Rev. Alexander Gilfillan. He was also to become the President of the Baptist Theological Seminary which Norman attended for a further three years. We had the highest respect for these men. We reveled in the knowledge that these men and the other part-time staff passed onto us from the Word of God. Our individual calls to mission work in the Far East coincided at this time.

Norman and I were married in 1961. We sought the will of the Lord for our lives. The direction was contrary to what we had expected but Norman has truly been the delight of my life and has taught me so much in the way of love and encouragement, his extroverted nature and natural love of people has been a joy to watch as he dealt with people.

Although we have experienced some of the hardest times, those journeys have been the most wonderful. Not only did we prove the ability of the Lord Jesus Christ during those times but our own marriage and love deepened.

During that time the Overseas Missionary Fellowship rejected us for service in Thailand. Our hearts were broken and it took some while to accept that God's timing was not ours.

We were 'called' to Sterling Baptist Church in East London, located in the Cape Province of South Africa in 1962. Norman was invited to be the Pastor. The congregation of Sterling Baptist Church was mainly returning 2nd World War Veterans.

The Baptist Executive of the Baptist Convention in South Africa told us that the members of that body had a unanimous conviction that God had placed a call on Norman's life to enter the Baptist Ministry.

Following that decision by the Executive many provisions were made for us by God in the form of support from individuals, to study at the Baptist Theological Seminary in Johannesburg, located in South Africa.

We were caretakers of a block of apartments. Norman did the repairs and I organized the staff as well as did the ordering of supplies for the apartments. Not only did we have this income but Norman was able to work as an electrician, for he had qualified for this prior to entering Bible College.

Grant our eldest son was born in Johannesburg during that time on May 3, 1962. We received such a wonderful gift as he came into this world bringing joy to all those in the apartments in which we worked as well as to the family!

That was the time to plant seed for the kingdom of God and a time when God began to uproot us as a family to fulfill that call to proclaim the Gospel to a lost and dying world. God called us to a Baptist church in Fort Victoria (now Msvingo), Rhodesia (now Zimbabwe) into the Baptist Ministry. This church was in a town over the northern border from South Africa.

Norman was ordained into the Baptist Ministry in 1965. Our other two children were born: - Caryn Ann March 20, 1965 and Hilton Craig Wood, February 26, 1967. Our joy was overwhelming as our family grew. The 'uproot' again of our family came as Norman was accepted into the army as a Chaplain in 1967. We moved to Salisbury, Rhodesia (now Harare).

The road to Rhodesian independence was inevitable, given the history of Rhodesia. The British, in the name of Queen Victoria had occupied Rhodesia. The capital, Salisbury, was named for her then Prime Minister, Lord Salisbury.

Cecil John Rhodes (Rhodes scholarship fame) initiated and exerted his influence upon what took place during the earlier period of the history of the country.

Settlers did not want the influence of Britain, 6,000 miles away, in their lives. This state of affairs continued throughout

Southern Rhodesia's history until the end of the Second World War. Many of the men in Rhodesia fought as allies of Great Britain. There were those that laid down their lives for freedom during that time. The bravery and dedication of Rhodesia's citizens were told in many epic stories. Almost all her citizens could claim British heritage.

Britain was economically weak by this time and she started shedding her colonies. There was however, a federation formed of Northern and Southern Rhodesia and Nyasaland.

By 1953, Southern Rhodesia could have had full independence. Instead the country voted again to join Northern Rhodesia and Nyasaland in a governing Federation for the common good of three independent countries. The majority of Rhodesians had voted for responsible government after being given the right to self-determination. They knew they had to live with the results of their actions in Rhodesia; they could not retreat to some other country.

Many missionary organizations played a large and important part in raising the living standard of those with whom they worked, to which the country owed a tremendous debt for the development of the country. The borderlands were given to mission organizations by Cecil John Rhodes for that purpose.

As late as 1957, the British Government was still committed to the concept of a federation. Then, within two years, the Monkton Commission was established by the British Government and was considering the question of secession.

Three years later, Nyasaland and Northern Rhodesia were given permission to secede but not Southern Rhodesia. In 1961, Sir Edgar Whitehead, the then British Prime Minister, negotiated a new Constitution for Southern Rhodesia . The Constitution was presented to the Rhodesian electorate and was accepted at a referendum with the promise that it would ensure independence for Rhodesia.

The promise of independence for Rhodesia however, proved untrue. In return for the assurance of independence, the electorate agreed to substantial political concessions to black Africans such as ownership of farms. Rhodesia maintained pressure on the British Government for independence. In September 1964, based on the majority of Rhodesians supporting independence.

In spite of an overwhelming vote by the members of the Federation in favor of independence for Rhodesia, Britain did not honor its commitment. A council of Chiefs and Headmen of the major tribes in all three countries also gave unanimous support to independence, but Britain again refused to honor the undertaking.

In June 1965, Rhodesia's traditional invitation to the Commonwealth Prime Ministers' Conference was withdrawn. It had traditionally been an open yearly invitation to all the Commonwealth members.

Independence was now imperative to Rhodesians. In October, 1965 the Prime Minister, Ian Smith went to London for what were described by the Commonwealth Countries as "final and conclusive talks" on the issue of independence for Rhodesia. Within a week these had broken down. The British Government reneged on its predecessor's Mr. Wilson's undertaking and declared that independence under the 1961 Constitution was no longer acceptable. Within a month the British Prime Minister was in Salisbury (Harare), and it was agreed that a Royal Commission consisting of members of the Commonwealth Countries be set up to determine whether Rhodesians as a whole would accept independence under the 1961 Constitution which had been established by the Commonwealth Countries. Rhodesians were thrilled with this significant breakthrough because of the promises that were made at the Conference with regard to the 1961 Constitution. Mr. Wilson the Prime Minister returned to Britain.

In the House of Commons, Wilson said his Government reserved the right to accept or reject the Commonwealth Countries Commission's findings - which included independence for the Rhodesian Government - an act tantamount to rejection of the Salisbury agreement which stated that independence was a foregone conclusion!

Rhodesians wondered what more was being required of them. Their country had proved itself economically viable. For 43 years stable self-government brought education, welfare and health facilities unequaled anywhere to the north in countries such as Zambia, Kenya, Malawi and others. Yet other African countries with nothing like this record of stability and education had gained their independence, sometimes with almost indecent haste such as Nigeria.

In November 1965 Ian Smith ceased the opportunity at this point believing that right was on his side to make sure that those who had built the country should have a say in the outcome of the country and declared UDI (Unilateral Declaration of Independence). The new nation of Rhodesia was born and would later die in 1980.

I visited Scotland with Norman which purpose was to present what was happening in Rhodesia. It was 1977, in the 25th year of Queen Elizabeth's reign and enjoyed the celebration of her Jubilee. We found Scotland a contrast to the wilds of Africa! Scotland was rich with beauty, history and culture. It is about ancient brave warriors, castles and legends. We also went to Northern Ireland, to speak about what was happening in Rhodesia.

# CHAPTER 2

**A war of terror ensued.** In November 11, 1965, the announcement came that Ian Smith, the President of Rhodesia, had declared a Unilateral Declaration of Independence from Great Britain. This led to fifteen years of war, which left indelible impressions upon us as a family.

Clifford Walter Dupont and Angus Graham (an British Lord by inheritance) conducted a commissioning parade where Norman had been attested into the Rhodesian Army July 31, 1967 as a class four chaplain with the rank of Captain. Both these gentlemen were contributors to the signing of the Unilateral Declaration of Independence document.

In 1977 on our visit to Britain we were able to see the ancestral home of Lord Graham. He had been one of the signatories to the new Constitution on Rhodesia. In addition we visited the British Parliament where the tour guide made reference to the fact that Lord Graham had been divested of his inheritance.

Norman facetiously told the guide he would personally report the fact to Lord Graham that he too was branded, as had been his forebears in Scotland in an earlier rebellion. The tour guide quickly retracted what he had said in reference to Lord Graham. All the Americans on tour with us cheered and clapped at this remark.

The events that followed the Declaration of Independence from Great Britain led to the deaths of thousands of Rhodesians both black and white. For a country the size of Rhodesia it was tragic.

During the years 1975-77 Norman (who was Chaplain General/Chief of Chaplains) conducted over a 100 funerals each year as well as about 100 weddings each year.

Christ was to prove Himself very real to us during that time. As a family we very rarely were able to sit down to a meal together. As a couple we slept an average of five hours each night. Usually in the early hours of dawn a 'sitrep' (Situation Report) would come to us and Norman would have to go and tell a family about the death of a loved one. Sometimes he traveled four to five hours to inform a family of the death or injury of a loved one. He became known as 'the angel of death'

*Prime Minister Ian Smith and Norman Wood*

As well as military personnel he often did the notification of the death of a civilian if they were serving in the army for periods of six weeks in the bush and six weeks at home. The war game became a game of 'hide and seek' with the terrorists hiding and the security forces seeking.

The terrorist infiltrated from Zambia, Botswana or Mozambique. The bands consisted of about twenty men. They were well armed. Their idea was to cause havoc on our mission stations. The land had been organized so as to have mission stations along the borders of Rhodesia. This was done by Cecil John Rhodes. He had been appointed to do this by the British Government.

# CHAPTER 3

Women at War. God provides *cycles* of life for us, each with work for us to do. Our response to those problems is important because we discover that, without God, life's problems have no lasting solutions! *Timing* is important. the secret to *peace with God* is to discover, accept, and appreciate God's perfect timing. The danger is to doubt or resent God's timing. This can lead to despair, rebellion, or moving ahead without HIS leading.

Is there a time for hating? We shouldn't hate evil people, but we should hate what they do. We should also hate the mistreatment of people, the starvation of children, and the dishonor brought to God. Most importantly we must hate sin in lives-this is God's attitude. Ecclesiastes 3:11 HCSB God has *"put eternity in the hearts of men."* We cannot be completely satisfied with earthly pleasures and pursuits. Because we are created in God's image we have a spiritual thirst, values and the realization that only God can truly satisfy us. We have a 'built in' restless yearning for the kind of perfect world that can only be found in His perfect rule. He has given us a glimpse of the perfection of His creation, but it is only a glimpse; we cannot see into the future or comprehend everything. Every thing is as God made it; not as it appears to us. We have the world so much in our hearts, and are so taken up with thoughts and cares of worldly things, that we have neither time nor spirit to see God's hand in them. The world has not only gained possession of the heart, but has formed thoughts against the beauty of God's works. We are mistaken if we think we were born for ourselves; it is our business to do 'good' in this life, which is short and uncertain; therefore we should realize that our time on this earth is limited and that we should do what we can when the opportunity arises.

During those years of war in Rhodesia as women we came to realize we could not change anything. How we responded to all these activities was the all-important factor.

As the nation of Zimbabwe came to birth (from the former country of Rhodesia, then Zimbabwe-Rhodesia) and after the election of President Mugabe and the Zimbabwe National Party in 1980 the question often came up from the opposing forces - "'what is the purpose of this war and how can a Christian be involved'?"

The women whose husbands were constantly being 'called up' or 'in the bush' were lonely and distraught. Out of the ashes of ruined lives, property and purposes, several good things came into existence. The Chaplain's wives became involved more and more in the day-to-day lives of the army, air force, and police wives. We worked in conjunction with Co-ord-A-nation an organization which helped those involved in practical ways. Canteens were started by the

Women's Voluntary Services to feed the men in camouflage as they came in from the 'bush'. In the forward areas, where the war was at its greatest intensity. Many farmers' wives opened their homes to members of the Security Forces for spells of rest and recuperation, providing baths, hot meals and a chance to relax. Women were also trained to cope with emergencies-everything from driving vehicles to fighting fires. Some of us helped in single owner businesses by looking after the offices when the men were 'called up'.

As Chaplain's wives we often went with our husband's on visits to the families who had lost someone in death. We would follow up with food and other help where needed.

The greatest part I played was encouraging the missionaries, farmer's wives, army wives, women at home alone in the remote parts of the country where access was difficult.

An incident took place on the way to Kariba in the north of the country on the border between Zambia and Zimbabwe. We stopped off in Karoi to have Bible Study and Services. We had with us the leader of the South African Baptist Convention, George Dennison by name. George had come specifically to encourage the people of Rhodesia (now Zimbabwe). The people assembled there had come at great risk to themselves because the roads were mined with anti-personal mines and the threat of ambush was very real.

During testimony time one of the families told of what had happened to them that week. They had been traveling in a small truck with three adults in the front and the terrorists began firing at them. After rockets and weapons stopped firing at them they all crawled out the front window which had fallen out and crawled behind a huge ant heap while the firing continued.

Once the army came through they found 6 rocket grenades fired and about 250 rounds fired at them and no one was hurt. When we asked them if they **believed** that God answered prayer they said they **knew** without a shadow of a doubt that God answered prayer because they had experienced it in that incident.

We had the joy as a family of sending Alfred, who worked for us in our home, to Bible School and then to see Alfred become a wonderful witness of the Lord Jesus Christ. It was our custom to give every one of our servants a Bible in the Shona language and then to encourage them to ask questions when they had read the Bible. Every morning Alfred would come in and ask questions about what he had read the previous night. We soon realized that the Holy Spirit of God was bringing Alfred to an awareness of his own need of a Savior. Along with a Shona evangelist we were able to lead Alfred to a saving knowledge of the Lord Jesus Christ. We asked him if he was willing to study for the ministry.

We laid down the condition that he would not leave the country but would minister to his own people. So many men were offered scholarships to study outside of the country all expenses paid and then they would never return. We told him if he felt God was leading him then he would be able to go and as a family we would support him. He came in a few weeks later to assure me that he would like to study for the ministry if we would consider sending his family along with him. We did so and a few years later his support was taken over by the mission to which he went as a pastor.

We heard many dreadful things which happened to him as he suffered at the hands of the terrorists. He had to hide his Bible under the ground when he knew they were in the area. His fearlessness was a constant challenge to us.

Norman spoke to another man Phineas, who worked for us in our home and asked him if he would like to enter the army. He did so and after his retirement twenty years later we received a letter from him in the United States to tell us that he was studying for the ministry and was going on to witness for the Lord Jesus Christ in the independent Zimbabwe. Not only did he face daily threats but he had such hardships that we cannot imagine. We know that in every way as we witness and become involved in the lives of the people to whom God calls us we will be assured that 'His Word will not return to Him void".

Farmer's wives often came to services that Norman conducted in lonely, isolated places where it was dangerous to go, some having traveled over 'anti-personal mined' roads and with the fear of ambush.

Many of these women slept in the passageways of their houses on the farms when their husbands were away following terrorists who had just brought havoc to their lives. These women were never written up as heroines. Several women became Air Force pilots, while others worked in support groups. Brave women came alongside the men with weapons to fight directly in a devastating war.

# CHAPTER 4

## The Saints

Our call to be involved with those known in the Rhodesian Army as the **Saints** (they adopted the hymn 'When the saint go marching in…" for their marching song), came when Norman was assigned to 2 Brigade of the Army as a Senior Chaplain. 2 Brigade, consisted of the Rhodesian Light Infantry, Special Air Service, Artillery and Armored Cars.

Rhodesian Light Infantry, was officially formed on February 1, 1961. In the latter part of 1961, RLI moved from Bulawayo to the new barracks in Salisbury having just returned from operations on the Northern Rhodesia-Congo border. In 1964 the organization and role of the Battalion was changed from a conventional infantry unit to a Commando Unit. There were three commando units and one support group.. The wearing of the 'green beret' was also introduced because they were an infantry commando unit and tradition in the

British army dictated that they were permitted to wear the 'green beret'.

Two Regimental traditions formed an important part of Regimental life, namely the "Regimental Quick march-The Saints", which was played on the bagpipes. They also had a mascot a Cheetah. From our home we would see the Cheetah take off after anyone on a bicycle. For many years the Regiment bore the brunt of border control operations against terrorist gangs that infiltrated Rhodesia.

We lived inside the barracks. As we heard the soldiers being marched past our house as a new intake of recruits came in for traditional warfare basic training, our prayer was that we would soon come to know them and introduce them to the Lord Jesus Christ.

Every week for the first six weeks of their training they were only allowed out to be with *us* for Bible Study in our home. Time after time we saw the results of the Holy Spirit at work in lives, that before were totally immersed in 'self' and now become concerned with others as they sought to do the WILL of God the FATHER.

Stories of the heroics of these young men can be read in the myriads of books written during the war years. We reminded them that Jesus Christ was the greatest hero. He came to this earth, laying aside His glory for them so that they might know Him whom to know is life eternal. The boys that came into the army to do their rigorous 'basic training' were men by the time they left.

Faces come before me even now as I think back on those days. The Holy Spirit is so powerful and we saw lives changed through the presentation of the Word of God.

We left The Rhodesian Light Infantry for Matabeleland where 1 Brigade was situated. Included in that Brigade were the Rhodesian African Rifles of who most were Ndabele. They were a proud, strong nation having their forebears in the Zulu of South Africa. They had a wonderful history. These were a brave warrior group of men having served in such places as Malaysia.

We returned to Army Headquarters in Salisbury (Harare) in 1972. The General of the Army, appointed Norman as the Chaplain General of the combined armed forces, that included army, air force and National Guard.

As Norman's arm of support in this ministry I spent the majority of my days, when not teaching at a private school for girls, in a car ferrying our children back and forth to music and extramural activities. Petrol (gas) was in short supply and we had coupons for the petrol. That entitled me to one trip a week into Salisbury (Harare) for these activities. In addition there were visits to those who had suffered loss or hardship during those times taking spiritual help and food.

Occasionally Norman was given extra petrol (gas) coupons for the fishing boat we co-owned with other chaplains. That was for 'rest and recuperation'. The boat was called "Sky Pilot". We had some special trips to Kariba, (at that time it was the largest man-made lake in the world) surpassed now by others. Kyle Dam was another place we visited as well as the Eastern Highlands of Rhodesia. We often faced the possibility of terrorist attacks and would have to carry weapons.

The Gideon International an organization that distributed specially marked New Testaments for soldiers were invited to the new army intake of recruits every six weeks. We were so grateful for the impact the Word of God had on the lives of these men as many of them when confronted by Jesus Christ accepted salvation in Him and began a new life with the Holy Spirit's help.

We heard of one such man - a Corporal (who had come to faith in Jesus Christ and accepted Him as his Lord and Savior). He was a soldier of 911 Battalion and was scouting ahead of his men. He had come to a viewing area which would be for a place to rest. That action, which, but for a few minutes, saved, the lives of the men on that patrol looking for tracks or any sign of terrorists because terrorists lay in ambush. When the Corporal came into sight via another route, the terrorists – ready for an ambush, fired, but expecting the soldiers to come from an anticipated route, missed every shot. One terrorist, however, with the use of a mortar managed to explode it about 15 meters away from the soldiers. The Corporal felt as if he had received a vicious blow to his chest. A piece of mortar, the size of a thumb nail, penetrated half way into his Gideon Bible then defected thereby lancing his skin about 7 cm and bruising his one lung."

Norman was constantly notifying families of the death of a loved one. On another occasion when he went to the Gerald

Parkin home to tell them that Gerald had been killed. His mother said she was pleased to meet Norman. Gerald had spoken so often of Norman and the 'Padre's Hour' in which Norman had the opportunity to introduce those young men to the Lord Jesus Christ. When packing his gear to go on maneuvers, Gerald's Gideon New Testament was always the last item-on the list in the bag and the first to be taken out.

# CHAPTER 5

## 'Suffering Saints and Spiritual Warfare'

Norman's testimony at that time was "having had the privilege of being a Chaplain for the duration of our present hostilities I can look back over the past years and say, without fear of contradiction, that there have been more miracles performed by God in this country of Rhodesia (Zimbabwe), over that period of time, than ever before in the short history of the country. Our Lord and Savior, Jesus Christ, has made Himself 'knowable' and 'contactable' through His Holy Word. As you read these accounts of miracles however, you will realize that the One we can contact and know and realize is the God of love and He is still in the miracle-working business, and humble thanks to our Lord and Savior and that He is the Almighty One working supernaturally in some cases to bring about His Will and the Will of the Father".

There are also miracles of the 'new birth' through the death, burial, and resurrection of the Lord Jesus Christ. Not one, praised God, but many, and we who had the privilege of living in Rhodesia, through its many years of pain and suffering we can look back and say with full assurance and say:- Ephesians 3:20-21 HCSB *"Now to Him who is able to do above and beyond all that we ask or think-according to the power that works in you-to Him be glory in the church and in Christ Jesus to all generations, forever and ever. Amen."*

During the years of 1965-1979 Christianity and Marxism were locked in a life-and-death struggle in Zimbabwe-Rhodesia. Overseas the secular and World Council of Churches were backing the men of violence.

Christianity seemed to be in retreat in Rhodesia (Zimbabwe). Ancestor worship was resurgent and the missionary work seemed to have been knocked back half a century – this had been established by Western Christians. Spiritual warfare was a reality for every Christian in Rhodesia both black and white.

Christianity still produced many saints and martyrs and as we remember them it reads like a chapter from Hebrews 12:1-2. HCSB *"Therefore since we also have such a large cloud of witnesses surrounding us, let us lay aside every weight and the sin that so easily ensnares us, and run with endurance the race that lies before us, keeping, our eyes on Jesus, the source and perfecter of our faith, Who for the joy that lay before Him endured a cross and*

***despised the shame and has sat down at the right hand
of the God's throne."***

Amongst this 'great cloud of witnesses' was a young black
evangelist called Bernard. On a February Sunday in 1979,
he was on his way to church when he was seized by terrorists
of the Marxist 'Patriotic Front' led by Joshua Nkomo, who
were backed and funded by the World Council of Churches.
Bernard was told "tear up your Bible or we will kill you". To
which he replied, "Let me read my Bible and say my prayers
and then you can do what you want." Bernard actually read
from his Bible to the terrorists and they allowed him to go
on his way.

Some of the evangelists were not as fortunate and were killed
for declaring their allegiance to Jesus Christ. Many paid the
'supreme price'.

We saw the grace of the Lord Jesus operative in the lives of
terrorists. One such was Pastor Musa who became a personal
friend. God alone could have worked the miracle in his life
at 'just the right time'. He was prepared with his commissars
to kill the leaders of the Christian church at a rally.

On that occasion he told his troops that when the 'altar
call' was made by the preacher at the end of the service they
were to go forward with their hand-grenades and guns to
kill especially the Christian leaders.

The Holy Spirit arrested him as he listened to the evangelist.
He never gave the order to his troops. He talks about his
present ministry being that of a reconciler. We do not

apologize for being either black or white but we should come as sinners to the throne of Grace, because Jesus came to die for all men. He was saved as a terrorist. His history was that he came from a religious background but although he knew about Christ he did not know the true Christ. He had a form of religion but he denied the Power thereof. He hated all white men and his greatest desire was that all white men should perish. In leading that group of terrorists to destroy the Church and Christian leaders, he personally, came to know the power of the risen Christ Jesus. He has replaced weapons of hate with weapons of love showing all men there is a place for them in the kingdom of God.

In March 1980, President Mugabe came to power through a rigged election, when people were made to put their mark twice on ballots and others were not allowed to vote because of physical restraint. There was so much of fear for the incoming Communist Regime in the hearts of people in Zimbabwe because they could not anticipate what would happen to the country in the future.

The second Sunday after the independence election I asked Pastor Musa to come and speak to my Teenage/Youth Sunday School class at the Central Baptist Church in Harare. I also invited our nephew Brian Wood into that class. Pastor Musa, a former terrorist, and Brian, who was based with the dog patrol in the Police anti-terrorist unit - came face to face. It was one of the most wonderful moments in my life, which will never pass from my memory. Brian was bitter and did not know how he would face Pastor Musa. I observed such humility in Pastor Musa and his words were "Brian you and

I would have been enemies under death prior to our 'new birth'. Now by the grace of the Lord Jesus Christ we are indeed 'brothers in Christ'. Brian made the comment to me afterward that had anyone come in to kill Pastor Musa he would have defended him.

During the course of the war, which lasted fifteen years, there were over 50 missionaries killed in Rhodesia. Many of these were personal friends of ours and had become vulnerable to attacks because the terrorists considered them as 'soft targets'.

The tendency to doubt God in times of trouble is the reaction of the human heart and we need to be encouraged to see it through God's eyes. Some heroes of the faith won battles, some were killed, but these were ***all*** commended for their faith. In June 1978, Rev. Jack Gardner, Norman, the pilot Chuck McDaniel of the Church of Christ mission and myself, made a visit by airplane to Sanyati (Southern Baptist Mission) to warn them of the presence of terrorists in the area. Just after our visit Archie Dunaway one of the missionaries from the International Mission Board of the Southern Baptist Convention was bayoneted to death by the terrorists - on June 15, 1978. Archie had been the one to take us to the runway when we left the mission. He thanked us for coming and also for the warning. Archie had also served elsewhere in Africa under similar circumstances.

For Norman this was a trying time because on June 23, 1978 the Elim Mission massacre took place. Norman felt responsible because he had recommended to the missionaries that they move from where they were to Eagle School thinking it would be safer for them.

Eight British missionaries:- three men and four women were brutally killed as well as their children numbering a total of thirteen. The women were raped, and all of them had been beaten and bayoneted. Also four young children were bayoneted to death - including a three-week-old baby. Mary Fisher one of the women missionaries, survived. She dragged herself into the bush despite her injuries and was found later by Security Forces. She was so badly beaten and bayoneted she died in Intensive Care three days later. Norman stayed at her bedside during that time.

Peter and Sandra McCann, both (30 years old) their children Philip 6, and Joy 5 years old. Philip (29) and Susan (35) Evans and their daughter Rebecca, 4 years old. Roy (37) and Joyce Lynn (36) and their three week old daughter, Pamela. Catherine Picken (55) Elizabeth Wendy Hamilton-White (37) Mary Fisher (28) Mary died after being in intensive care in the hospital.

Norman and Peter Griffith, the head of the Pentecostal Holiness Mission wept and had several weeks of sleepless nights.

Later one of the terrorists who perpetrated these murders was converted. He said that the reason for his conversion was the manner in which these missionaries died. He could not get that incident out of his mind. The Holy Spirit of God hounded him until he surrendered to Christ. He is not allowed into Zimbabwe and is evangelizing in other parts of

Africa. He is telling those who would listen that only God could forgive him.

Rural blacks suffered the most. Several thousand men, women and children died. Christians were hounded out and slaughtered. Many suffered such merciless torture, raped and violated and then were wounded or killed. The only way Christians can look at such violence is through the eyes of the Sovereign Lord otherwise life is meaningless.

# CHAPTER 6

## "Inside the Fortress"

**Ephesians 6:12 HCSB** *"Our struggle is not against flesh and blood, but against the rulers, against the authorities, against the powers of this dark world and against the spiritual forces of evil in the heavenly realms."*

Zimbabwe takes its name from ruins which are located at the town of Fort Victoria (now Msvingo), a short distance across the border from South Africa. The Zimbabwe Ruins are fascinating and mysterious. They are one of the 'seven ancient wonders' of the world.

We were called to the ministry of the Fort Victoria Baptist Church where Norman served as the pastor. That was prior to going into the Defense Force. During that time we would often spend time out wandering around the Zimbabwe Ruins on our visits there. Some of the mystery lies in the fact that no one seems to know who it was that built the fortress.

Kyle Dam, another beautiful place for water sports and fishing. It was located in the Zimbabwe Ruins area. We would go to cottages which had been built by the army for 'Rest and Recuperation' of the battle fatigued soldiers.

After one such occasion, Norman was in the Operational Center at Army Headquarter on the Monday following our visit. He called me to say that within hours of us leaving the cottages terrorists had attacked and one of the cottages was destroyed by fire. God was so good to us in those days with the protection that constantly surrounded us.

The war in Rhodesia was not just a military struggle; it was also an economic struggle. There were United Nations sanctions; there were no imported luxury goods, or food including necessary items, such as gasoline, cars, machinery, weapons, clothing, literature, and technical products.

The constant psychological and spiritual pressures against Rhodesia was the intended goal of the United Nations and other countries to bring the country into subjection.

When Harold Wilson of Britain imposed sanctions on Rhodesia in 1965 he said the 'rebels' in Rhodesia would be 'brought to heel' within a few weeks. But Wilson was so wrong. Ironically, he did as much for Rhodesia's economic development as did Ian Smith the Prime Minister.

The landlocked little colony was forced to diversify her economy and to embark upon an ingenious program of substituting imported goods with local goods which had been improved upon for consumption. From 1969 to 1974

Rhodesia's economic development was far more impressive than Britain's. Breaking sanctions which had been imposed by Britain became a way of life. Planeloads of Rhodesian beef went to the tables of all the African presidential palaces. The shared railway system between Zambia, Botswana and Rhodesia was a symbol of economic interdependence.

Breaking the imposed sanctions extended to Britain, France and other countries. Rhodesian businessmen broke the sanctions and continued trading with Britain, France, and even a number of Eastern bloc countries such as Eastern Germany.

We endured all sorts of product shortages; pantyhose, razor blades, evaporated milk, chocolates, and luxury goods were in short supply. Anyone who went to South Africa on vacation would come back laden with goods unobtainable in Rhodesia. We loved the South African chocolates, fruit drinks, and clothing.

In 1974 the economy began to suffer. Oil prices quadrupled and other products became very expensive. Portuguese rule in Mozambique came to an end. The most important factor, which contributed to the economic squeeze, was the fact that the escalating war was costing the Rhodesians one million American dollars a day.

A narrow view of what was happening in world events was inevitable as we were cut off from the rest of the world. Secrecy surrounding the war effort was intense as there was infiltration amongst the general public by the terrorists for the purpose of finding our how trading was carried on during the imposition of sanctions.

Another problem was instead of traveling on one's own there were convoys of vehicles traveling within the country, they became vital for everyone traveling as there were guards and soldiers with weapons making the safety and security of everyone a matter of top priority. In the front of such convoys there was often a vehicle which was equipped with landmine detecting apparatus an invention which was later used for other vehicles.

As Christians the spiritual security and heroism we portray is in our personal relationship with Jesus Christ, The inner strength and security of the Christians during this time was amazing to see.

Some of the heroes were from the farming areas of Rhodesia (now Zimbabwe) who constantly lived in fear of being attacked either with weapons of war or landmines, - on the roads, at home or on the farms. Norman was witness to many of these heroes as he conducted services in these dangerous areas to which the average minister would not or could not go.

Until the war; Rhodesia/Zimbabwe had been so possessed with materialism. Zimbabweans became aware that we were all in the war together. Selflessness became a way of life for all the citizens.

# CHAPTER 7

## "Roll of Honor"

My memory goes to July 17, 1983 when the Garden of Rest (which was a wall which housed the ashes of those that had died in the conflict in Rhodesia) dedicated at Selous, a farming area just outside of Salisbury (now Harare). The couple responsible for not only the Garden of Rest but also for the building of the Chapel at Selous, was Dan and Muriel Cloete. They were farmers in the area and all four sons as well as their Dad were in the Defense Force during the conflict in Rhodesia. They did everything in that area to maintain a Christian witness. In addition they wanted a memorial to remain for those that gave their lives for their country. We could always go out to their farm for rest and recuperation from all the trials that surrounded us at that time.

The farmers including the Cloete's have since had their lands seized by Mugabe the President of Zimbabwe. In some of the family events they have barely escaped with their lives. One of the sons, Colin who headed up the Farmer's Union (an organization which set standards for imports of food from the farming districts) has suffered incarceration and when bail was posted he continued to work for the farmers. The land since 2002 had been devastated which caused starvation and exorbitant food prices.

Muriel Cloete's sister Doris Lappin and her husband Tommy (both deceased) were also the friends we needed at that time. They stayed at Lake Kariba, we were able to go and rest and recuperate from the stresses of life under terrorism. At one time Kariba was the largest man-made dam in the world. It was a beautiful spot with a lot of history in the making. The best times were when we went out on our boat 'Sky Pilot' a boat in which many of the Chaplains had shares. As the sun would be setting it was a beautiful sight to see the elephant crossing from Fothergill Island back to the mainland with the sun behind them. On one such occasion we were privileged to see a little trunk sticking up out of the water and when it got close to the mainland a baby elephant emerged.

Our last wedding anniversary before we left Zimbabwe in 1980 was spent at Kariba. Our favorite hotel there was called Bumi Hills which was only accessible by plane or boat. We were able to go there and I shall never forget this wonderful land. We could go at any time and unwind from all the stress and strain of those days.

On one occasion Norman conducted a baptismal service in a pool at Kariba Dam. There were 10 people baptized who had surrendered to Christ and became Christians. It was a glorious service and to again see that the cross had not lost its power to save men and women. We were enthralled to see the Holy Spirit at work in the lives of men and women.

On another occasion while we were in Kariba there was mortar bomb attack from across the border of Zambia. It occurred at the conclusion of a wedding. There was only one injury during the time that the bombs were falling. When Norman went to the hospital and introduced himself to the nurse on duty she asked if there was an Xray technician at the wedding. When Norman asked the injured person for permission to pray for him he replied that he did not believe in prayer to which Norman's response "I do and just be quiet while I pray." He then made his way back to the reception and made an announcement to the guests "is there a doctor in the house and a X-ray technician". Immediately a young man and his partner responded. They were transported to the hospital whereupon Norman walked into the room where the patient was lying and said "you don't believe in prayer? And I do here is a doctor and an X-ray technician to care for you and it is time you started believing in the Almighty God. To which the patient replied "Amen!" Another miracle from the hand of God.

We praised God for the individual lives that witnessed such times of danger and the deliverance from those dangers. The love and compassion of Christ came through ministry to those who did not know Him as Savior and we saw many come to faith in the Lord Jesus Christ. Kariba was close to the Equator and very hot. It was so hot during the summer that the asphalt would melt at the airport. The hot air would rise causing air-pockets. On another occasion when Norman came in to land in a 'Tail Drag' Cessna Airplane piloted by Chuck McDaniel the plane began to bounce down the runway as a result of the air pockets. Our friend Tommy Lappin who was the fire chief and controller at the Kariba airport was trying to help Chuck to bring the plane in to land. Tommy could be heard broadcasting to say;…"clear to land…..to land,… to land… to land…." because the hot air caused the plane to rise and eventually they came to a halt!!!!

Many were such visits to Kariba for Norman with the pilot Chuck McDaniel who was a missionary with the Church of Christ. He offered his services to take Norman to the places that were normally inaccessible. Shell Oil sponsored such visits by supplying free gas. Hallelujah! Another one of God's miracles.

Some of the human examples of sacrifice were honored in the Rhodesian war by ceremonies to grant medals of Honor. A Senior Game Ranger Willem Marthinus De Beer was given a medal for brave and gallant conduct over and above the call of duty on May 2, 1972 while a crashed helicopter from which he had escaped was on fire, one of its gas tanks exploded and he returned to a blazing wreckage and released the pilot who was trapped inside by his safety harness. During this action, the second gas tank exploded, and although he would have known of the probability of this occurring, he continued his efforts to rescue the pilot and carry him to safety.

In juxtaposition to the bravery and sacrificial love of these brave people is the love of our Savior, Jesus Christ, Who not only died for His friends but also for His enemies. No other religion or faith can point to such an awesome example of sacrificial love. The Cross of Christ, where His life was shed for us in His death of our Savior on our behalf - stands supreme!

On November 11, 1978 Norman was awarded the Defense Forces Medal for Meritorious Service by the Acting President of Rhodesia. It was given for devotion to duty in the Rhodesian Army. That medal represents the many hours that were spent counseling, performing duties, weddings and funerals. He performed a hundred funerals and a hundred weddings each year during the years of 1975-78.

The strain upon family relations was great and when family problems arose he was never home and the leadership in the home fell to Maureen. There were eight months of the year when Norman was away in the operational field. What amazing times these were as the Lord led us into a ministry to provide spiritual and social needs for families. We visited the wives and families and ministered to their needs as the Lord directed us.

God's 'Roll of Honor' extended to those who did not get the recognition of a medal. But were rewarded with the "Well done you good and faithful servant"..from the Savior.

Bill Dodgen (became the second in command to Norman) and his wife, Beverley was on call, day and night, and the 'sitreps' (Situation Reports) came fast and furiously. Bill and

Beverley faced so many personal trials with the death of their little girl of two years who suffered with cystic fibrosis. She died during their vacation in South Africa. The family returned to Salisbury with the body. It was heartbreaking for that family as well as the family of Chaplains.

Bill took the reigns when we left Rhodesia as Chaplain General/Chief of Chaplains.

Lancelot Dikito a black Chaplain who was killed in a vehicle accident, followed Bill as Chaplain General. He was sadly missed.

Val Rajah, an Indian followed as Chaplain General after the death of Lancelot Dikito. I have mentioned him later on and what he did during a time when there was destruction of airplanes and the trial that followed.

There were Chaplain's assistants who were important to the Corp. of Chaplains. Their involvement was on a part-time basis. They responded when they were needed. They were preachers in their own individual congregations. Tribute is paid to them because of the dedication to service and to the One whom we serve the Risen Lord Jesus Christ.

One such man was Mike Rutter. He showed little interest in spiritual things until he was involved in a land mine incident where he was blown up into the sky and when he landed he had some serious injuries which required hospitalization. While under observation it was discovered that he had polycystic kidneys which was hereditary. Norman spoke to Mike in the hospital and challenged him about the fact at

God had spared him, and asked him what he going to do with his life.

Mike accepted the challenge and surrendered to Jesus Christ for service. He became a Baptist Minister in Zimbabwe and South Africa. He is a kidney transplant recipient.

Stan Hannan came to Norman's office and asked for the opportunity to serve the Lord Jesus Christ in the army's Chaplain's Corp. Six weeks later he approached Norman as to what had transpired with his request to serve. Norman said to him "are you serious?" to which Stan replied "Yes!". That night he was on the train to Llewelyn Barracks in Matabeland to the south of the country for basic training.

Stan had been saved out of a background of 'show business'. He had managed a 'pop' group 'The Four Jack's and a Jill'. The production of "A Chaplain's Story' and "Rhodesia Unafraid" was his initiative. Norman shared along with other Chaplains and telling the story of what chaplains did in their day to day lives.

More than once the farmers wives would come to services traveling on roads just after a landmine had exploded. Their husbands were on follow-up of the terrorists. Wherever services were conducted, people in the rural areas would come and every available seat was occupied. The reverence and awe that everyone felt during those services was heavenly. Death was a reality with which we lived every day. Vigilance and faith went hand in hand. The 'times and seasons' saw many changes due to the war. Family life in particular became very precious.

One of the events that remain in my mind was when the President of the South African Baptist Union, George Dennison, visited Rhodesia. He came to the country prepared to share the Word of God with us. He said he learned so much as he saw how people displayed simple trust and faith in the Lord.

We were on our way up to Kariba. We stopped off in Karoi as Norman had been scheduled to preach there during a weekday evening. We went to a house which was packed out with people many of whom were standing outside. Suddenly the lights went out. The service went on as though nothing had happened. The local people remarked "Oh! I suppose they have blown the power lines again". No one moved. The presence of the Lord was so real.

A man nicknamed 'Tiny' gave his testimony. He told how during that week he and his family had been on their way into town. As they came out onto the main road, lights began to wink and 'Tiny' suddenly realized that it was rifle grenades and trace bullets. Whereupon the front tires were blown and the truck came to a standstill. Three adults and a child sat in the cab. They scrambled out of the window of the cab. A miracle in itself as both men weighed over 250 lbs each. The one man dragged 'Tiny's' wife out and ran to an anthill for cover. Willie grabbed his little girl and made a dive for the other anthill. When the security forces came by an hour later they discovered that the terrorists fired 250 rounds of ammunition and at least 10 rifle grenades had been fired. The family reported no injuries. When Norman asked "Do you believe in miracles?" He replied "no! I ***know*** He performs miracles"

George came away from there with his heart full of praise to God. There were so many circumstances and personal testimonies of God's deliverance and power.

# CHAPTER 8

## Exit and Entrance

Ecclesiates 3: 7 HCSB "Says; ...*A time to tear and a time to mend, a time to be silent and a time to speak*"

'The Herald' newspaper of Zimbabwe dated, Saturday February 16, 1980, printed so many conflicting reports about the terrorist war situation in Zimbabwe. Some reports were of the security forces winning the conflicts and in others the Security Forces of the present government were loosing the conflict. Norman and I had been to the Bank in downtown Salisbury (now Harare) and the streets were cordoned off because of a bomb scare. At the Catholic Cathedral a bomb was dismantled.

There were no meetings or public rallies allowed in Melsetter a city located in the Highlands of Rhodesia. The governor issued warnings of new outbreaks of terrorism; these appeared to be senseless given that there were peace talks between the government of Rhodesia, Terrorist leaders and Britain in progress. In the middle of this disturbing page in the newspaper the British representative for the Queen of England, Lord Soames was assuring the electorate that when the voting took place for the elections he could assure all the parties at the peace talks that there would be a free and fair election as people went to the poll to vote for the new government.

Those of us who had endured fifteen years of terrorist warfare had doubts as to whether this would ever happen. The past had proven that reneging on the part of the British was part of the history of the long years of war that we had endured.

In January of 1980 it had become evident to Norman and I that Zimbabwe-Rhodesia was on the verge of collapse. There were elections coming up and we were certain that Mugabe would be the victor. In March the victory was his. The day Mugabe won the elections was an infamous day. I had been writing examinations at the technical college down the road from where we lived. During the examination I could hear the cheering and noise as Mugabe's warriors with the 'Cock Cry' of jubilation made me aware he had won. When I came out of the examination room there were Rhodesian Light Infantry soldiers on the corners of the street trying to ensure the safety of citizens.

Our eldest son, Grant, had been drafted into the army that day for his basic training. I was devastated not only that our son was to enter the military on the day that Mugabe won the elections but by the elections themselves. I could not believe that all this was taking place around me. Norman had insisted that Grant enter basic training if we were to encourage others in Rhodesia to accept what was happening.

That evening Norman went out to be with a friend who was very ill. Our friend died during the course of the night. On his return home Norman got into bed and it was then that I had the most amazing vision. I was not given to visions. I saw our friend Andrew van den Aardweg, a Chaplain in the South African Defense Force signaling to Norman to come over and help South Africa. Andrew had been responsible for leading Norman to a saving knowledge of the Lord Jesus Christ in Rhodesia and he had since moved to South Africa. I had argued in the vision with Andrew saying Norman had had enough of war and trouble. Andrew had this very large set of wings like that of an eagle on his chest. He held up a shield and he said the South African military wanted us to go to a camp in Simonstown as Norman was in danger.

In my quiet time before the Lord the next morning I had read from a devotional book 'The Living Light' dated March 6, 1980. I could not believe what I was reading. Deuteronomy 1:33 HCSB says, ***"The Lord God...went with you on the journey to seek out a place for you to camp. He went in the fire by night and in the cloud by day to guide you on all the way and selected the best places for them to camp, and guided them by a pillar of fire at night and a pillar of cloud by day".***

I woke Norman in my excitement and told him of my vision. He was not too enamored because of the lack of sleep. He did however, get up and go to work. During the morning the telephone in his office rang and it was Andrew van den

Aardweg was on the line telling Norman that they were making arrangements for him to get out of the country as they had heard broadcasts out of Mozambique and Tanzania to the effect that he would be killed. We knew that God alone was in control of the situation.

I was warned that same day by an army officer, who had come from a meeting where the military and the new government representatives were present, that Norman would be 'killed' if he continued to ask Mugabe to answer questions, such as "…what would the role of the Chaplain be now that you have come to power? For you, Mr. Mugabe to come to power there were fifty missionaries killed and I would like to know if this persecution will continue? Also you used to broadcast out of Tanzania and Mozambique and make statements such as "down with Jesus Christ His mother is a whore". He apologized and said that he was not aware that this was happening. Norman knew he was lying. There had been harassment and physical abuse of the Chaplains and Christians by his Commissars.

When the soldiers came to take Bibles from the Chaplains. The Commissars would knock the Bibles out of their hands. The reply by Mugabe was not sufficient to encourage us to stay in the country when he said; "That is war and in war there are casualties. The other thing you must expect Chaplain General is that you will include 'tskwero' (witchdoctors) in the Corp. of Chaplains and you can begin to accommodate that in your thinking". "Norman replied: "I could not accept that responsibility." To which Mugabe countered that his usefulness to the country had now ended.

This could not be acceptable to us as Christians so we began the process of leaving the country.

In June 1980, we came upon a meeting in a hotel with the army officers and British officials who were instituting a hand over to Mugabe. Norman had conducted three funerals that day and then in the evening there was a wedding in a hotel in Salisbury. We had been back and forth to the hospital where Norman's mother lay close to death. It was obvious that here were the men who had 'sold our country down the river'. One of the Generals came over to greet us. I could not talk to him I was so disgusted with what had transpired over the past months. Ian Smith the former Prime Minister had been put to the side.

None of the things promised by Mugabe were implemented and the British did nothing to force his hand. Political opponents, including Ian Smith and Joshua Nkomo, co-operated with the government and Mugabe used that to his advantage. Once he gained the strength he needed to govern, he dispensed with these two men. Now Mugabe began to show his true colors. He worked gradually until he had a 'one party' state in Zimbabwe and then he declared himself to be the President.

The "North Korean" model was the method he used in dealing with anyone who opposed him. He used intimidation, murder, torture, and atrocities. Mugabe had an increasingly chronic sense of insecurity. He has been driven by power, wealth, prestige and a sense of his own importance. During the election in 1980 Mugabe guaranteed – the right to strike, - freedom of the press, - free speech, - freedom to form and organize trade union, - freedom of procession. freedom of association, - freedom of worship.

After the election Mugabe abrogated all these promises. One of the first acts of control was to muzzle the free press and he did this by the dissolution of the local Guild of Journalists and replaced it with a new association of his appointees. They were affiliated to the international journalist trade union organization with head offices in Moscow.

Whatever the reasons for the split between the two major tribes (Shona-Mugabe and Joshua Nkomo- Ndebele), it was catastrophic. Killings in the south of the country resumed. The effect of Nkomo's humiliation and the arrest of the two ZIPRA (Joshua Nkomo's political party) generals was to anger and alienate the Ndebeles (people group).

Suspicion deepened between the two major tribes and their respective political representatives. When the killings in the countryside resumed suspicion deepened. In a situation of increasing insecurity and tension, all "neutrals" were once again suspect, whether missionaries, white farmers, tourists, or Airforce officers they were liable to be eliminated. Chaos ruled from this time forward. One example was what the Zimbabwean's call "A night to remember". This was Sunday, July 25, 1982. At 3.10 am. the Air force base at Thornhill came under attack. 7 Hunter aircraft acquired in 1962 were destroyed, 1 Hawk a brand new aircraft and a Cessna 337. Damage was done to another Hunter and 3 more Hawks. The explosions damaged offices and buildings. In most air forces a disaster of this magnitude would be regarded as more than unfortunate – almost half of the country's operational war planes were incapacitated, but as for Zimbabwe is was disastrous.

The result of the findings after the Air force officers had suffered and been released was that the perpetrators of the attack had come from South Africa. All the senior officers of the raid were not from within Zimbabwe. The accused officers from Rhodesia were mercilessly tortured by the 5th Brigade (N. Koreans) until they gave confessions of a plot to destroy the Air force. But they had never been involved, They were namely:- Air Commodore Philip Pile, The men arrested unjustly were; Air vice Marshal Hugh Slatter, Wing Commander John Cox, Wing Commander Peter Briscoe, Group Captain Jones, Barrington Lloyd, were well-known to Norman as part of his coverage as Chaplain General (Chief of Chaplains) was not only the Army, but also the Air force, Police, and all other units.

The Chief Justice Enoch Dumbutshena, who headed up the trial, was a Christian. He was fair and stirred up public opinion to get the truth presented to the world despite the pressure on him. In the end these men were acquitted of all crimes. With a huge crowd gathered waiting for them to be released these men were re-detained by Herbert Ushewokunze.

Val Rajah who was then the Chaplain General was given the task telling wives the bad news of the detention order. There was no possibility of a trial to look forward to and only long dark days of imprisonment. At this time all of them came into a personal relationship with the Lord Jesus Christ. Due to a reporter misquoting some remarks Val made, he was suspended. He went ahead and organized services for the families and prayer meetings, which lasted for all the years that the airforce men were held on re-detention. He was reinstated after 82 days.

Mugabe had decided to release the re-detained men because of overseas pressure from England and the United States. Mugabe succumbed to the pressure mainly because he was visiting London to get money for Zimbabwe.

Val Rajah is worthy of mention at this time because of his wonderful testimony. He had contact with Norman when he was drafted into army and sent to Llewellin Barracks, in Bulawayo which is in the south of the country of Zimbabwe. He was saved from Hinduism in 1965 and by 1972 when National Service (draft) was made compulsory by the Rhodesian Government he went to the Commandant Lt. Col. John Thompson and asked permission to have services with the Colored (mixed blood from black and white parentage) and Indian National Service who were 'billeted' there. The next Sunday he went in and set up at a spot where the Colored (mixed blood) and Indians were billeted. He used to take Gary his son with him-he played the trumpet and Val played the guitar. That was when he contacted Norman. Norman wrote letters and got to the officials involved and was able to bring Val into the Chaplaincy as the first non-European non-African to be commissioned into the Defense Force as a Captain in the Chaplains Corp. Eventually Val became the Chaplain General/Chief of Chaplains for a few years after we left the country.

### *Our FAMILY After June 1980:*

Our Family unit disintegrated:-Grant and his then fiancée Janette went to Virginia in the United States to Liberty Baptist University. When they returned to South Africa from the United States they were married in Zimbabwe.

We moved to the Navy in Simonstown, Cape, South Africa, where Norman went into the navy as a Chaplain. to the Free Church in Simonstown. We also were responsible for the the Free Church in Da Gama Park, a naval cantonment. Caryn and Hilton went to Treverton Baptist School in the Natal Province of South Africa.

Two years later Mondeor Baptist Church, Johannesburg called Norman as pastor. Mondeor Baptist Church was the nearest church to Soweto, the black township, that became the center of the activity that would later result in the downfall of 'apartheid' in the country. The wedding of our daughter Caryn to David Wayne Fenwick took place in the church.

In 1985 we came to the United States for Norman to preach "Revivals" (preaching for several nights) in Alabama. In 1986 Eclectic Baptist Church sponsored us to come to the States and in one of the churches where Norman had preached Revival the church called Norman to become their Pastor. We spent four years at Tallaweka Baptist Church in the Tallassee area. It is located between Montgomery and Auburn.

Hilton our youngest son came with us from Africa. After graduation from college he trained to be a radiology technician. He became the manager of the Vaughan Regional Hospital, Selma, Alabama. He is now in Texas with his wife Isa where both of them are working in a hospital in Dallas, Texas. His daughter Meghan, came with us on a mission trip recently to Germany and Scotland. We took her and our youngest granddaughter Lara, after spending time with the Fenwicks in Berlin to Scotland with us to see the country where her grandfather was born and that was a great time we had with her. Meghan is now doing her Master's degree in psychology. She is hoping to go into clinical psychology when she has completed her Master's.

Caryn and Wayne graduated from the University of Mobile. Amey Maureen Fenwick was on the way and at their Commencement Ceremony Caryn was pregnant. They had to return to South Africa to await the process for the 'green card'. they had two and a half years to wait. Amey was born in America and was three months old when they returned to South Africa. Lara was born on their return to the United States. They spent four years at the Georgia Baptist Children's Home as Care Givers. The Fenwicks became American Citizens and Wayne served as Student Minister at the First Baptist Church, Monroeville, Alabama.

Wayne and Caryn left Monroeville when they were accepted by the International Mission Board of the Southern Baptist Convention to serve in Berlin, Germany.

1990 we were called to Daphne Baptist Church in Baldwin County, Lower Alabama. We served there for two years.

The International Mission Board of the Southern Baptist Convention contacted us and asked us to go to Tokyo, Japan. Our eldest son Grant and his wife Janette with their two girls, Christie-leigh and Samantha asked us to make application for them to come to the States. Janette died of cancer in January 2008. Grant and his two daughters visited us in Japan. It was wonderful to have them. We went to Disneyland in Japan and they were fascinated that the bears spoke Japanese. They also experienced their first earthquake while they were there. Their comment after the earthquake was cool..." What a delight it was for us to be together. Grant has a high-powered job and is remarried. Yolanda is a wonderful companion to his two daughters. Christie-leigh (our eldest granddaughter) and Michael, her husband were married and have one son our third great grandson Brayden and she is expecting her second son. Samantha is studying Veterinary and living in Houston, Texas.

# CHAPTER 9

## Japan

*'We are not doing right. Today is a day of good news. If we are silent and wait until morning light, we will be punished. Let's go tell the king's household." 2 Kings7:9 HCSB*

This is the title of a sermon Norman preached from 2 Kings 7:1-11 & 16 in which he pointed out that the 'sin of the church is that we are silent' about our faith. The first point in this amazing story about 4 lepers who were *amazed* at what they found' when they got to the Aramean camp' everything had been provided by the Lord. The second point was that they were *absorbed* with what they got in vs.8 the church is so taken up with programs and activities that we become absorbed with what our church is doing. The third point of the sermon was that they were *ashamed* at what they had done verses:9-10 and so they became vocal. They told the thousands in the city who were doomed about God's provision in and through His Grace.

As Christians we have so much more than that to speak about. Emmanuel 'God with us' has become the reality that 1.6 billion people in this world have never heard There are 3,052 unreached people groups in this world. Japan is a country possessing its own unique beauty and is blessed with a climate and terrain of astonishing variety-from northern areas where snowfall measures over ten meters (33ft) in winter, to tropical regions. Japan is divided by a backbone of mountain ranges, covered by a variety of vegetation, and has many lakes, swift-flowing streams, and fertile plains well suited for cultivation.

Japan has always been blessed with an abundant supply of resources from the sea. Freedom from invasion in the past enabled it to preserve its own distinctive culture, and thanks to a natural setting that is mild, rich in seasonal changes, and blessed with the fruits of the mountains, fields, and seas, its inhabitants were able to create a unique culture. The seasonal variation in Japan's plant life inspired not only the art of flower arrangement (ikebana), but also the sense of impermanence that was infused into the spirit of so much of their life such as the tea ceremony (cha no yu), gardens and other parts of their lives. Because so much is based on the seasons there are numerous festivals and customs which reflect the seasons.

Japanese handmade paper, one of the most durable papers in the world. The houses are visually separated by paper-covered doors, without cutting them off from each other completely, by allowing an appropriate amount of light to enter from outside. Bonsai are used as an art of creating miniature potted trees, now widely practiced all over the world.

Asia has over half the world's population, only two percent are professing Christians. That number amounts to thousands upon thousands that have never heard the name of Jesus.

Christian history dates as far back as 1549. Francis Zavier the Catholic Jesuit missionary came. In 1582 however persecution took place through Hideyoshi. Twenty-six martyrs were executed on crosses in Nagasaki.

During the Tokugawa Shogunate there was a special police commission organized whereby Buddhist priest were required to report whether or not any Christians were known to live in their area.

In 1853 Commodore Perry arrived. Japan's ports were opened to foreign ships and within four months, seven Protestant missionaries landed. Yokohama had the first Protestant church. Believers were drawn mainly from the samurai and upper middle class. The period 1883-1889 was marked by rapid growth of the Protestant Church.

## THE SILENT MAJORITY BECAME
## THE VOCAL MAJORITY

Norman was called as Senior Pastor of Tokyo Baptist Church, Japan in 1992. The leading to the church was nothing short of miraculous. We had been approached by a visitor in the church at Daphne, Alabama to give us a tape of the sermon that Norman had preached. The message was on Caleb, found in Joshua 14: HCSB Caleb was one of the two spies that went into the Promised Land. He and Joshua came back with a report that God would be able to conquer the inhabitants. The other ten spies were so negative about the 'giants in the land'. The tape had been sent to Tokyo Baptist Church; at the same time the International Mission Board approached us to consider Tokyo. We had looked at the profile and decided that we were too old.

However, the International Mission Board requested a tape of one of Norman's sermons be sent to them which they in turn let the church have the tape. When the church heard the second tape they were overcome by the leading of the Lord.

We had no doubt that God had called and that God would equip us despite our age. We became missionaries serving with the International Mission Board of the Southern Baptist Convention. For eight years we served in Japan. For six years we served in Tokyo and 2 years in Yokohama. The six years in Tokyo we witnessed tremendous changes not only in the missionary strategy but also in the church. There over 50 different nationalities in the church at any given time. We had over those years up to 80 different nationalities that visited us.

After people had been saved they were immediately asked to serve. The evangelism team became very effective in every outreach ministry. One of the most effective ways to reach the vast population was on the circular rail system which traveled around Tokyo. Those that had been prepared to witness got onto the Yamanote Line train and handed out fliers and literature and also they would pick a station on rotation and stand to witness outside the station to those millions coming and going on the transit system. We taught various workshops such as 'Share Jesus without Fear" and the "4 Spiritual Laws" in both English and Japanese so as be able to equip the members for going out into 'the world to make Jesus Christ known.'

On arrival in the church the emphasis in the Weekday Ministries changed from that of cultural ministries to Bible Studies. Including the Wednesday night Bible Study and Prayer Meeting there were eleven Bible Studies in the church with many Bible Studies and Prayer Groups in homes.

During our time there we witnessed over 350 baptisms in the church. All of the converts were asked to do some form of witness training. They returned then to their 'home' countries many of which did not allow missionaries into their countries. Nigerians, Ghanians, Filipinos, and Malaysians, went to pastor churches.

Wedding Anniversaries, birthdays, and other special events that the church members put on for us, will always stand out in our memories.

Marriage Enrichment held every Saturday evening. Once a year we would have a Retreat for the married couples at Amagi. It was the Retreat Conference Center, which was run by the Japan Baptist Convention given to them by the

Japan Baptist Mission. Our greatest thrill in the church at Tokyo was to see how many people were called out into ministry.

After a Revival with the President from Beeson School of Theology, Dr. Timothy George, there were fifteen people that surrendered at that time to go as missionaries throughout the world. When Norman counseled them, many were encouraged to study at the Theological Seminary in Tokyo. Others went to various other places as missionaries after a time of study for seminary students. They were people from all over the world. Our friends came from so many different nationalities and denominations. That kaleidoscope of nationalities and people groups still take my breath away as I think on the many wonderful things that God did during that time.

One young lady had graduated from university in Tokyo as a doctor decided to minister to people who had cancer and other diseases which were terminal. Her father was a very distinguished official of the police was so perturbed by this decision. Timothy George offered her a scholarship to study in Alabama, USA with a specialty emphasis. Her desire was to be able to give comfort to those who did not have any hope in this world. Her Savior Jesus Christ was so real to her having come out of Shintoism and she wanted them to have the opportunity to be introduced to Jesus Christ her Savior.

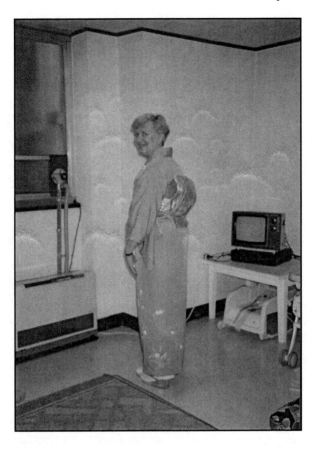

The women's meetings that resulted from the various requests from so many nationalities also revealed the divergence of Bible Studies. There were Precept Ministries and videos, Bible Study Fellowship groups, Beth Moore's studies and videos, International Bible Studies, Japanese groups, and other nationality groups as well. In all the ladies Bible Studies constituted eleven groups.

One of the most wonderful things that happened to us was with one of the many visitors we had in Tokyo, Margaret Wood came to visit us. Her testimony follows: - "In December 1998 I flew from Johannesburg to Tokyo to spend three weeks with Norman and Maureen. I was relating how difficult my life was. Norman chipped in as I described my situation and said why did I work there when I was so unhappy in that work situation. I replied that as I was my sole source of income, I had no option to have to work.

Norman said we had not been created to live like that, and if I lived another thirty years how awful it would be. Norman asked me what I would really like to do and I replied that I would like to start a 'Bed and Breakfast' for Christians to be able to rest and recuperate and be with their Lord. These two folk, Norman and Maureen encouraged me to step out in faith. I went into Norman's office in Tokyo Baptist Church and typed out my resignation.

On March 1, 1999 I arrived in Durban, South Africa (on the coast of Natal) to look for employment and a house. Within two weeks I had employment with a sugar farmer. This was just the setting for me to think and pray for the future. There were birds singing outside my office windows and many animals in view from that window as well.

I was led to a house which became my home and to this day I recall the miracle of God's provision in such a real way. This house was the Bed and Breakfast home I had always dreamed about. I have entertained many of God's children and been able to provide them with the rest they need. A conversation started in Tokyo and later confirmed while I was still in Japan with Norman and Maureen at a Baptist Retreat Center on the Izu Peninsular." From Margaret Wood

For the next eighteen months we ministered at Yokohama International Baptist Church. God again worked in such a wonderful way the congregation going from 70 to 200 members. Many ministries were started there. These ministries were to the Homeless, Men's meetings, English, Bible Cells and working with the language missionaries.

# CHAPTER 10

## Retirement

Our official retirement date from the Japan Baptist Mission became effective on November 1, 2001. We had thirteen months of 'Home Assignments' during which time we had the unique opportunity to be in some of the greatest churches in the United States. We saw the work of the Holy Spirit in evidence. Churches that were Mission-minded and came alive not only numerically but they were sending over 80% of their membership on short or long term Mission trips.

The Lord again called us into the 'fields, which are white unto harvest'. This time we went to Antiqua one of the Leeward Islands; in the Caribbean. Antigua is a small island of 108 square miles. As the largest and most developed and heavily visited of the British Leeward islands it has grown into a very successful tourist center. The Antiguan International Baptist Church is in the capital which is St. John's. The capital has a population of 36,000. It is located at the mouth of one of the island's natural harbors. Together with Barbuda (28 miles to the north) and an uninhabited rocky islet name Redonda, they form the independent nation of Antigua.

The church was to be set up for autonomy, an International church by nature. On our arrival we were distressed by the fact that the missionaries were expected to do everything in the church. The Membership consisted of people who had simply been invited to join the church without any consideration of whether they were born again or not. The result was that it was a complete shambles. After due consideration Norman made the statement during a morning service that if there were people in the church who had not accepted Jesus Christ as Savior and who had not followed the Lord through the waters of believers baptism they were no longer members of the church. This caused consternation but brought about the cleansing of the church. It was then that the church began to grow. Men and women were eager to study the Word of God and to witness to their new found faith in Christ.

God in His wisdom and power brought circumstances to bear on us that changed the dynamic of the church.

My mother Agnes, went with us to Antigua. She fell and broke her hip in three places and her shoulder in two, she had surgery and then six weeks later, because the rehabilitation after surgery had not been successful we had to return to the States as there was no one in Antigua who could redo the surgery.

Concurrently with this event, Norman lost his sight in his right eye through a stroke behind this eye. Medically this problem was call a 'Central Retinal Vein Occlusion' and his eye deteriorated. The doctor in Antigua recommended that we came back to the States to seek further help from an ophthalmic retinal specialist as soon as possible. After Norman saw the specialist in the United States it was recommended by our International Mission Board of the Southern Baptist Convention that Norman should return to Antigua and close down the mission.

Norman was able to do all the legal work to enable him to hand over the property to the Antigua International Baptist Church in a very short time. A leader was appointed to help bring the church to autonomy and to function as a body. The leader was an Antiguan with Canadian citizenship.

On our return to the States we did an interim pastorate at East Point Baptist Church for almost two years. It was truly a wonderful experience and the church has gone on to become a very large, active church.

We moved to Florida at the beginning of 2005. Since coming to Florida we ministered for 4 years in Lake Ola Baptist Church (now 1st Baptist Church Tangerine) in Zellwood, Norman was the Pastor of the church.

The next lap of our journey has been to King Street Baptist Church. This church is on the Space Coast of Central Florida. Those who started the church were employees of the Space Station and now many of the people in the original church have moved away.

In September 2012, we went to Haines Creek Baptist Church in Tavares, Florida area. The church has the most wonderful Care Center ministries which is well organized for those in need.

Looking back, we've traveled to many countries, met people from all walks of life. There has been a lot of good times but also hardships and sometimes we were in areas so dangerous we didn't know if we would ever get out alive. God met with Abraham and encouraged him. In the words of ***Genesis 15:1 HCSB ...Do not be afraid, Abram, I am your shield; your reward will be very great..*** Throughout our ministry we have been motivated by the fact that we wanted Jesus Christ's Name to be held in high honor in all that we did for Him.

CPSIA information can be obtained
at www.ICGtesting.com
Printed in the USA
FFOW01n0640020215
10769FF